CHINESE EROTISM

CHINESE EROTISM

Presented by
Marc de Smedt

Translated by

Patrick Lane

Miller Graphics

We are indebted to the French Natio-
nal Library, Paris, for exceptionally
granting us permission to reproduce
the documents on the following pages :
2, 7, 11, 12, 15, 17, 18, 21, 23, 25, 27,
29, 31, 32, 35, 37, 39, 41, 43, 45, 47, 54,
73, 74.

Reproduced by permission of the Ins-
titute for Sex Research, Inc., Indiana
University, Bloomington, Indiana,
USA : 5, 8, 9, 10, 14, 16, 20, 22, 24, 28,
34, 36, 38, 40, 42, 48, 49, 51, 52, 53, 56,
57, 58, 59, 60, 61, 62, 63, 64b, 65, 66,
67, 68, 69, 70, 71, 72, 76, 77, 78, 79, 80,
81, 83, 84, 85, 86, 87.

We also wish to thank Mr. Lawrence
E. Gichner, of Washington, for allo-
wing us to reproduce the documents on
the following pages : 6, 30, 46, 50, 64a,
82, 88, 89, 90, 91, 92, 93, 94, 95, 96.

The extracts from the *Sou Nu King* are
reproduced with the kind permission
of Editions Seghers/Robert Laffont.

Designed and produced by
Productions Liber SA

First English edition published by
Production Liber S.A.

I.S.B.N. 0-517-351102

This edition is distributed by Crescent Books,
a division of Crown Publishers, Inc.

a   b   c   d   e   f   g   h

© Productions Liber SA
Fribourg - Genève, 1981

Printed by Printer Industria Gráfica SA
Provenza, 388 Barcelone, Espagne
Depósito legal: B. 36149-1980
Printed in Spain

Of being enraptured by the Jade Stalk...

Introduction

The people of ancient China were fond of making love. They saw it as way of harmonising the energies of heaven and earth and thus of continuing nature's cycle of creation. So love became an art, the art of living, the art of untying the body's knots. It was also an integral part of religion. Thus, to the great indignation of their enemies, the Taoists combined sexual practices with their techniques of meditation. This should not surprise us, for they saw Tao as a vast and unbroken stream of energies whose movement reflects the totality of the cosmos. The energy of Yin and Yang is everywhere at work, and each human being has a twofold nature, masculine and feminine. The union of these two principles creates life, thus the *Tao* goes on unceasingly. Sexual energy remains the greatest transformative force, being involved directly in the

great dynamic interplay which is the basis of the physical world and the rhythms of nature. So at a very early date treatises appeared in which sexual positions and techniques were described in practical terms and with a wealth of detail. One essential point emerges from them, that the man should not waste his energy and, in a polygamous society, should satisfy several women for the sake of domestic peace. Thus ejaculation was to be avoided at all costs, as it tired the body, and as far as possible orgasm was to be reached only rarely. The main satisfaction centred on pleasurable physical contact, positions and the richness of shared experiences.

The Taoists quickly realised that techniques for retaining sperm were extremely effective: not only did the man thus avoid dissipating his energy and the woman achieve climax, but a subtle alchemy was wrought between them. The male took the

It is natural,
The game of creation,
The game of life,
Everywhere.

woman's Yin and she profited from her partner's pure Yang nature. He is Yang, she Yin: the Yang sets the Yin in motion, which in turn releases more Yang. Conversely the woman's Yin activates the man's Yang, which releases more Yin. Both partners can draw sustenance from this exchange. The woman should have as many orgasms as possible so that, in accordance with the laws of heaven, as much Yang as possible be produced. The man should be as sparing as possible with his sperm so that his ancestral Yang energy does not escape and his vital energy retains its intensity and longevity. This does not prevent ancient authors from asserting that the man should achieve orgasm from time to time, to make conception possible, obviously, and also to release his tensions and enable him to dissolve in the crucible of shared orgasm.

Amongst many ancient texts on this subject are to be found *Sou Nü King* and *Su Nu Fang*, in which the legendary Yellow Emperor, *Huangdi*, is seen receiving his sexual education through the sexual expertise of young women. These treatises on sexual initiation, from the 4th century A.D. at the latest, were not the only ones: amongst the rest are to be found the *Yu Fang Mi Ju* (Secrets of the Jade Chamber) and the *Dong Xuan Zi* (Son of the Mystery of the Grotto). Extracts from these four treatises accompany the delightful illustrations to the present work.

According to all the treatises it is beneficial to make love as much as one can and as far as possible into old age: "A man, even an old one, does not wish to be without a woman. If he is without one, his concentration *Yi* is disturbed; if his *Yi* concentration is disturbed, his *Shen* spirits are weary; if his spirits are weary, his longevity is reduced." And we read elsewhere: "The purpose of sexual intercourse is to balance one's energies, to set one's heart at rest and

Night has come,
Let us fall to the games of love
In the bedchamber.

to strengthen one's will. Next follows clarity of mind *(Shen Ming);* the person concerned feels a deep sense of wellbeing, an absence of heat and cold, hunger and satiety, the body being totally at peace. The outcome to be desired is orgasm for the woman and for the man preservation of his strength."

The Taoists were well aware that women are sexually more vigorous than men, just as water is stronger than fire. Certain texts even say that a woman can enjoy lovemaking more than eight times. Consequently a man can exhaust his strength with a woman. If he uses retention techniques, both can harmonise Yin and Yang and experience the "Five Heavenly Pleasures". If he does not, he dissipates his potency and will die before his time.

Sexual relations should best begin with gentle play which harmonises the lovers' energies and attunes their emotions. When their passions are fully roused, coitus can take place: The Jade Stalk, Red Bird, Pillar of the Heavenly Dragon, or in other words the phallus, enters the woman's Open Peony Flower, Vermilion Gate, Golden Lotus, or Hidden Vessel. Slow penetrating movements alternate with sudden thrusts in groups of 3, then 5, then 7, then 9. Positions vary, thirty being proposed. They are the same as are to be found in all cultures, with a few variations.

In all these techniques deep breathing and deep exhalation play an important part as a means of retaining control and calm. The importance of relaxation before the sexual act was also emphasised, and all the texts insist on the importance of establishing total harmony with one's partner, of exploring the other's body and its sensitive zones, caressing it, showing one's adoration and drinking from the "Jade Fountain".

The purpose of intercourse is to balance the energies, set the heart at rest and strengthen the will.

But these pieces of advice for lovers should not make one overlook the ultimate goal of sexual intercourse: the "Fire Pearl", depicted at the dragon's side in all Chinese art. This mysterious jewel is the perfect symbol of Yin-Yang energy unified, pure vital energy condensed from primordial cosmic energy. It may be that in coitus the hidden parts of man's being open out like a flower, enabling him to "see his own face as it was before birth". That is to say, one can go back to one's roots, melt into the "Valley of the World", into the fertile void which is pure energy or *Ch'i.* For as we read in Lao Tseu's *Tao Te King:*

"Clay is moulded into vases, but their use depends entirely on the empty space within."

Marc de Smedt

Those who do not know the Way think that lovemaking can harm the health. In fact the point of love is not only diversion or bodily pleasure, it can also calm the heart, strengthen the will. Then both body and spirit are at peace.

Su Nu King

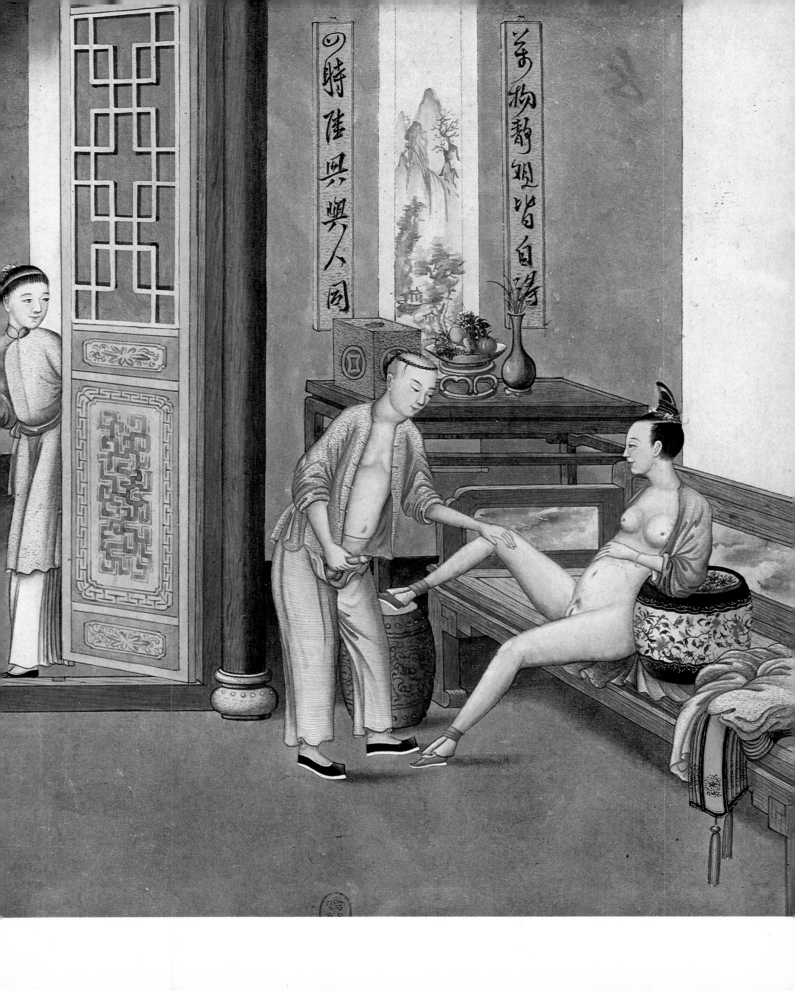

Giving the woman her orgasm and avoiding weakening the man, these are the goals to be desired.

Sou nu king

Huangdi, the Yellow Emperor, asked *Sunü* (White Girl): "I feel a lack of energy and a disharmony of body, I am sad and often afraid. What can I do about it?"

Sunü replied: "All men make a mistake during the sexual act. Women conquer men as water conquers fire. Those who know the art of love are like those who can mix five different flavors in the cooking pot to produce a good meal, like those who know the way of Yin and Yang and enjoy the Five Pleasures. Those who are ignorant of this art die young and thus taste less of the pleasures of life."

She added: "I know a person, *Cainü,* who has the secret of *Tao*."

The emperor sent *Cainü* to ask *Pengzu* for the secret of longevity and was given the answer: "A man must retain his sperm and also take medecine. If he is ignorant of the art of love then all is in vain. Men and women are like the earth and the heavens, they are destined to unite and are also eternal. If a man does not understand this art, he dies young in consequence. When

Space and time disappear
In the caves of the spirits,
Pain and joy disappear
On the shores of our Fortunate Isles.
                                                    Kin P'ing Mei

a man has grasped the art of Yin and Yang, the way of immortality opens up before him." *Cainü* thanked *Pengzu,* bowed deeply many times and then took her enquiries further: "I would like to know the nature of this art."

Pengzu replied: "The method is simple, but often people do not have the willpower to follow it. The present emperor rules the earth and has no time to follow all the techniques. Fortunately he has many concubines, so if he follows the right method for intercourse he will feel light in body and his troubles will disappear. The essence of the matter is to have intercourse with girls without ejaculating."

Sunü reported to *Huangdi:* "When facing the enemy it is best to think of him as trash, a stone or tile, whilst seeing oneself as jade or gold. When one unites with a woman, one must feel like a rider on a galloping horse moving along the edge of a deep chasm studded with upturned dagger-points. If you can manage to retain you sperm, you will live for ever." .

16

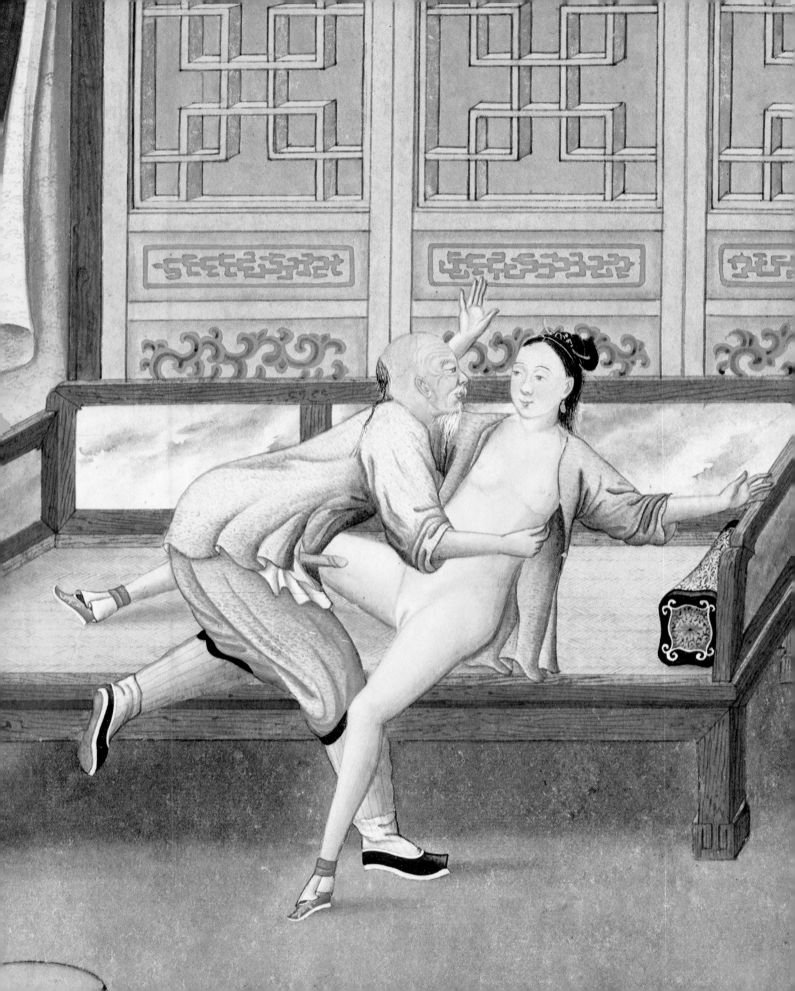

Know the mascu-
line,
Cleave to the femi-
nine,
Be the Ravine of
the World.
Whosoever is the
Ravine of the
World,
Virtue will be his
constant compa-
nion,
He will find his
youth again.

Lao-Tseu

Two bodies united
Breathing as one.

19

Love knows the art of adorning itself with artificial charms for the great game of love.

Huangdi asked: "What will happen if one abstains from sex?"

Sunü replied: "That is absolutely out of the question. Yin and Yang have their variations, as all things have. Man is as subject to the law of Yin and Yang as he is to the changing of the seasons. Without coitus *Shen* cannot blossom out, Yin and Yang are pent up, for how could they be invigorated in such a situation? If the person concerned does breathing exercices to eliminate the old and absorb the new he will indeed be invigorated. If the Jade Stalk (penis) is inactive, it will perish. It must be activated by the *Tao Yin* method, which consists in motion without emission. This method, called *Huang Jing* (Reversal of Semen), is a technique for prolonging life."

Huangdi: "What are the elements which bring about the perfect union of Yin and Yang?"

Sunü answered: "For a man the essential point is to avoid weakening his strength. For a woman the important point is orgasm. Those who do not follow the method will decline into weakness.

The aim of coitus is to balance one's energies, to set one's heart at rest and to strengthen the will *(Zhi)*. Then comes clarity of mind *(Shen Ming)*. The person concerned feels a deep sense of wellbeing, an absence of heat and cold, hunger and satiety, the body experiencing pleasure in peace.

The outcome to be desired is the woman's orgasm and the preservation of the man's strength."

Men belong to Yang.
Yang's nature is to awaken swiftly
But also to subside easily.
Women belong to Yin.
Yin's nature is to awaken gradually
But also to be slow to achieve satisfaction.

Huangdi enquired of *Xuannü* (Black Girl): "I have learned the technique of Yin and Yang and would like to know the reasons behind it."

Xuannü replied: "The union of Yin and Yang is necessary for any kind of movement in the universe. Yang is transmitted when it comes into contact with Yin; Yin changes when it seizes Yang, for Yin and Yang are complementary. Thus the male organ becomes hard and the female opens up, the two energies are united and both sperm and female secretions begin to flow. Men have to observe eight stages, women eight palaces. If this rule is not followed, the male will be affected by *Ju Yong* and the woman will have difficult periods; other maladies and eventually death will result. Those who follow this rule will always have a shining countenance and long life."

Huangdi asked: "What does one obtain by practising coitus according to the way of Yin and Yang?"

"For the man the purpose of coitus is to generate energy; for the woman to avoid physical disorders.

Those who are ignorant of the method think that coitus harms the health. In reality the sole purpose of coitus is bodily diversion and pleasure, also to calm the heart and strengthen the will. Because of it one feels one feels neither hunger nor satiety, neither heat nor cold. Body and spirit are both at peace.

Energy enters and leaves the body in a gentle, steady flow without any feeling of desire disturbing the harmony; that is the effect of this kind of intercourse. If this rule is followed, women can obtain complete orgasm and men enjoy perpetual good health, "replied *Sunü*".

The man should retain his sperm and avoid ejaculation. Thus he absorbs the energies of the woman's Precious Gate by drinking her saliva. This pratice brings good health and a long life.

Ta-Lo-Fu

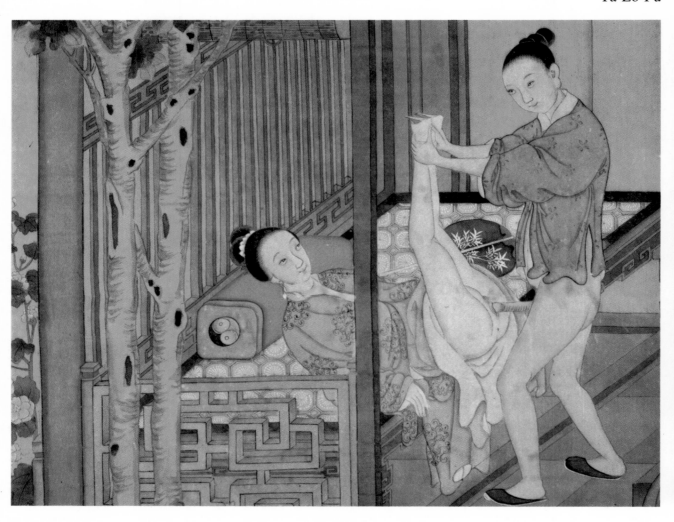

The way of Yang is simple. It suffices to be relaxed and not to hurry.

Yu Fang Zhi Yao

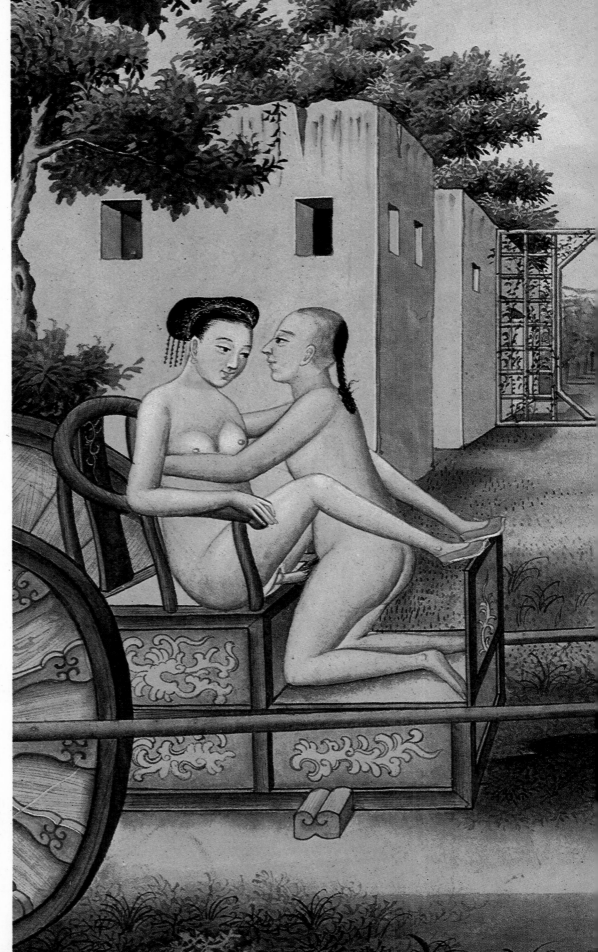

The way of coitus lies first in caressing and charming one's partner so that her Shen *(spirit) is at peace, then in intercourse.*

No medecine, no spiritual aid can prolong a man's life if he neither knows nor practises the Tao of love.

Peng Tsu

Huangdi put another question: "Just now I would like to make love, but my Jade Stalk will not rise. My face shows the depth of my shame and is covered with beads of sweat. Yet my desire is so strong—what would happen if I helped it with my hand?"

Sunü answered: "The problem Your Majesty has mentioned is a simple one. When a man wishes to make love to a woman, certain customary preliminaries must be observed. First harmonise the breathing, then the Jade Stalk is aroused according to the law of *Wu Chang* and emotion floods the Nine Parts. In the case of women, five colors are to be noted. According to the color, the man collects saliva from the woman's mouth which in turn is transformed and fills the marrow of his bones. The prohibitions of *Qi Sun* (the Seven Deficiencies) must be obeyed, the way of *Ba Yi* (the Eight Benefits) followed and the laws of *Wu Chang* observed. If all this is so, energy strengthens the body and cures all disorders. The internal organs are harmonised, the complexion shines and when desire appears, the Jade Stalk fills with strength and becomes erect, whereupon the enemy surrenders. Where then is the shame?"

28

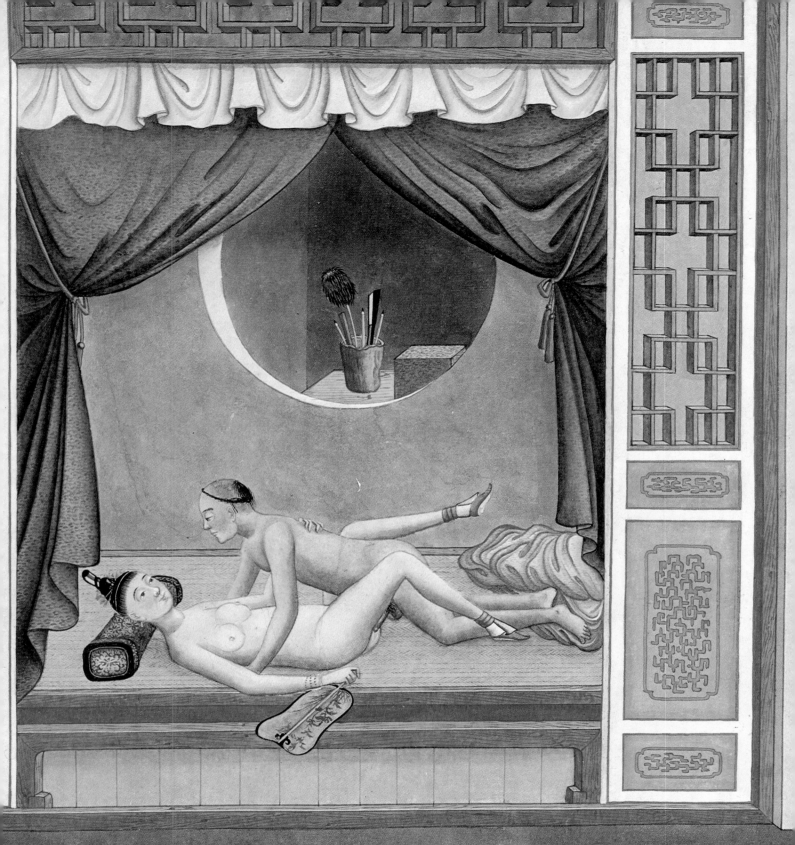

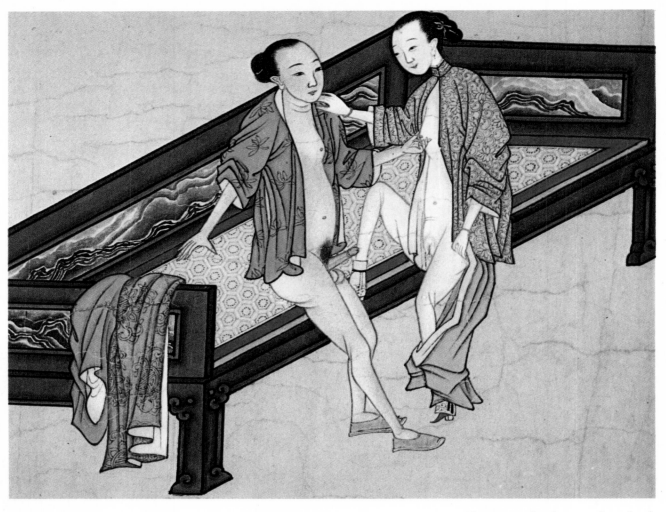

If you make love a hundred times without ejaculation, you will have a long life.

Sun Sû-Mo

Huangdi: "If during intercourse the woman experiences no pleasure, her secretions do not flow and the Jade Stalk does not rise, what must be done?"

Xuannü: "Yin and Yang are interdependent. If Yang lacks Yin it is unhappy; similarly if Yin lacks Yang it cannot move. If the man desires intercourse but the woman does not, or vice-versa, their hearts are not in accord; if there is roughness and brutality, Yin and Yang will not interreact.

When desire is mutual, the two emotions unite; the sexual organs of the woman tingle, the Jade Stalk is full of strength and erects. The Jade Stalk touches *Shu Shu,* penetration takes place fast and slow by turns. *Yu Hu* (the Jade Gate) opens up and the secretions flows, all without any need for force. The woman absorbs the semen which strengthens the energies flooding into *Zhu Shi* (the Red Chamber).

I propose to Your Majesty five rules to be followed: *Shen* (stretching), *Suo* (withdrawing), *Fu* (bowing), *Yang* (rising), *Qian* (moving forward), *Que* (withdrawing) *Qu* (stooping) and *Zhe* (bending)."

30

The salt breeze
Rises up from the sea,
The wind of pleasure
Rises up from desire.

Huangdi: "Is really such a thing as the method of Yin and Yang?"

Xuannü: "Of course. Before making love to the woman, ask her to lie on her back and to bend her legs. Then the man positions himself between her legs, kisses her mouth and sucks her tongue. Then he touches the east and west side of the Gate with his Jade Stalk to enter it. If the Jade Stalk is large it penetrates to the depth of a measure and a half, if it is slender, to the depth of a measure. The Jade Stalk does not rotate but simply advances and withdraws, but see to it that it does not slip out, for that would lose the beneficial effects which eliminate disorders.

When the Jade Stalk enters the Jade Gate it generates heat, the woman rotates her body and the man penetrates deeply. This action has the power of banishing all maladies.

It is also possible to do things in a different way: first touch *Qin Xian* (the Lute String), then insert the Jade Stalk to a depth of three and a half measures nine times with closed mouth. Then penetrate as far as *Kun Shi* while inhaling in front of the woman's mouth. Do the same nine times, or nine times nine, which is to say eighty-one."

Pengzu: "After ejaculation the man's body feels utterly fatigued, his hearing is diminished, he is sleepy, his throat is dry and his joints feel wrenched. Of course he has experienced a certain amount of pleasure, but only for a brief moment. Moreover he has not felt true pleasure. If he does not ejaculate, his strength increases, his hearing is sharpened and his sight is clearer. Thanks to an effort of will and self-control his body feels better—so how could one possibly think that he has not experienced pleasure?"

Huangdi: "I would like to know the effects of intercourse without ejaculation."

Xuannü: "Intercourse without ejaculation strengthens the energies. After intercourse twice without ejaculation, one's hearing and sight improve. After three such experiences all physical disorders disappear. After four, *Wu Shen* (the Five Spirits) are at peace. After five, the blood and the blood-vessels improve. After six, the back and the lumbar region are strengthened. After seven, the pelvic area is reinforced. After eight, the body glows. After nine, the man will live for ever. After ten, he can converse with *Shen Ming.*"

I entering my mistress,
She feeling me enter,
Sweet moments for us both...

O to enter from the rear
Love's sweet opening!

Huangdi: "How can you tell that the woman is experiencing orgasm?"

Xuannü: "There are five signs, five desires and ten movements. The Five Signs are:

1. Her complexion becomes flushed: at this moment the man should kiss her gently.

2. Her breasts harden and perspiration appears on her nose: now the Jade Stem should penetrate slowly.

3. Her throat becomes dry, and she swallows: now the Jade Stalk moves gently.

4. Her vagina becomes slippery: now the Jade Stalk penetrates deeply.

5. Her secretions flow down to the perineum: now is the time to penetrate and withdraw gently.

The Five Desires are:

1. *Yi* (thought): she breathes rapidly.

2. *Yin* (vagina): her mouth and nostrils are wide open.

3. *Jing* (quintessence): she hugs her lover.

4. *Xin* (heart): her perspiration wets her garments.

5. Desire for orgasm: her eyes are closed and her body stretched out.

The Ten Movements are:

1. Hugging her partner in such a way that their genitals touch.
2. Moving her thighs so that they rub against her lover.
3. Tightening and expanding her abdomen to speed up her partner's enjoyment.
4. Rotating her buttocks to increase her pleasure.
5. Hooking her legs over her lover's so that the Jade Stalk can penetrate more deeply.
6. Pressing her thighs together as orgasm begins.
7. Turning on her side when she wants her partner to penetrate deeper and touch both sides.
8. Pressing her body against her lover's is the sign that orgasm is increasing.
9. Stretching her body is the sign that orgasm is filling her whole being.
10. Her vagina becomes slippery, pleasure has reached its climax, orgasm has taken place."

Why search for the Elixir of Immortality
when you can drink
from the Jade Fountain?

Hsu-Hsiao-Mu-Chi

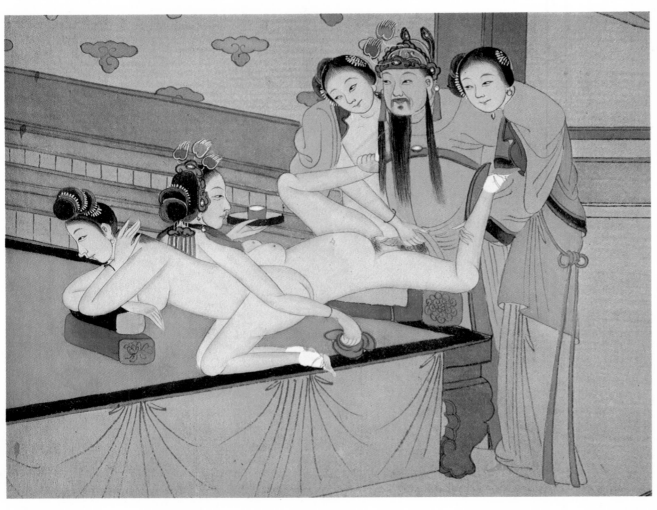

To say that a thing is good or bad simply because it seems so to us amounts to saying that nothing is good and nothing bad.

Tchouang Tseu

Huangdi: "If someone loves sexual intercourse but his Jade Stalk will not erect, can it be made to do so?"

Xuannü: "Certainly not: for men the way of coitus needs the Four Arrivals and for women the Nine Energies."

Huangdi: "What are the Four Arrivals?"

Xuannü: "If the Jade Stalk will not erect, it is because the energy of harmonisation has not arrived. If it rises but it is not big enough, it is because muscular energy is missing. If it is large but not hard enough, osseous energy is lacking. If it is hard but not hot enough, it is because *Shen* energy has not arrived.

Erection is the *Ming* (light) of quintessence; swelling is the *Guan* (barrier) of quintessence; heating is the *Men* (exit) of quintessence. The Four Arrivals of these energies are decided by the *Tao* (way, path, reason...). One must be fully conscious of what one does and avoid

Before leaving on a journey
The lovers frolic
One more time.

The great secret of love is to be able to control one's ejaculation even if one is passionately roused by one's partner's beauty. Inability to control oneself leads to sickness and debility.

Wu Tzu Tu

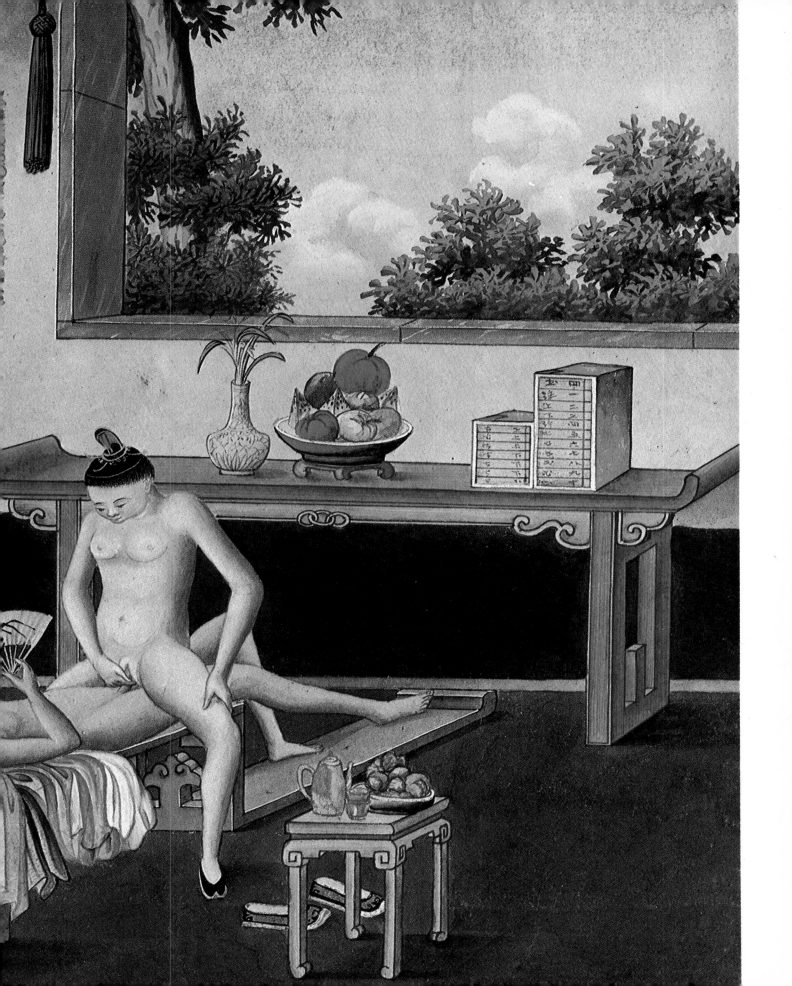

Beyond a doubt walls can have ears
And no window is safe from prying eyes.

Kin P'ing Mei

ejaculating during intercourse."

Huangdi: "Very well. But what are the Seven Energies?"

Xuannü : "When a woman finds it difficult to breathe and has to swallow frequently, it is because her pulmonary energy is coming through. If she hugs her partner, this is a sign of splenetic energy. The slippery vagina shows the arrival of renal energy. If she puts on airs and affectations, it is a sign that osseous energy is flowing. When she caresses the Jade Stalk, her sanguineous energy is at work. When she strokes her lover's nipple, her carnal energy has arrived. If intercourse is to last for a long time, all these energies must be experienced, otherwise physical disorders could arise later."

Cainü: "The greatest pleasure in sexual intercourse is ejaculation. If one does not ejaculate, how can one experience this pleasure?"

46

Dongxuanzi: "Before ejaculating, the man should wait for the woman to achieve her climax, whatever he himself wishes. Once she has done so, he can ejaculate, withdrawing the Point of Yang to place it between *Qin Xian* (the Lute String) and *Mai Chi* (the Teeth of Wheat) and as far in as a nipple enters the mouth of a baby at the breast.

The man must immediately shut his eyes, position his head immediately above his tongue, press his shoulders together, stretch out his head, open his nostrils, close his mouth and inhale. In this way the man can limit the amount of sperm emitted in each ejaculation, restricting it to two to three tenths of a normal ejaculation.

To conceive a child one should have intercourse after the cycle. A child conceived on the first and third days after the end of the cycle will be a boy, on the second and fourth days after the cycle it will be a girl, and five days after the cycle conception will be impossible. The man must wait for the woman's orgasm before ejaculating, and she must lie on her back, close her eyes and concentrate on absorbing the sperm. *Lao Zi* also says that a child conceived at midnight will have a long life, conception before midnight will ensure a life of average length, but a child conceived after midnight will live less long."

> *Their boisterous behavior made them look like a playful pair of*
> *young Phoenix or lively fishes wriggling in the water.*

> Kin P'ing Mei

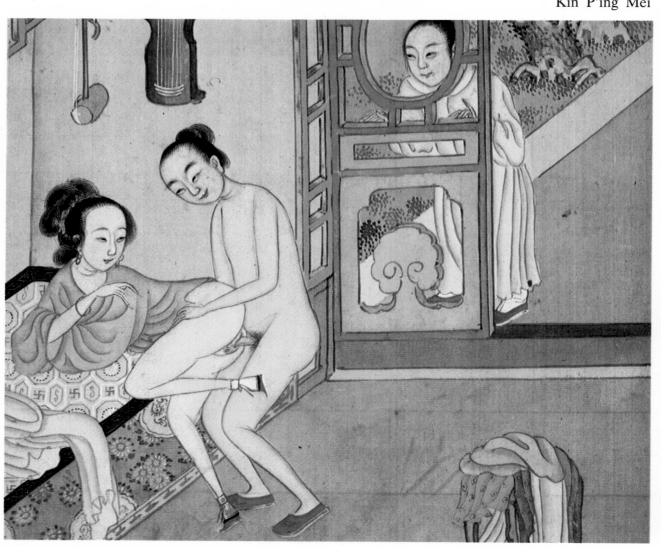

He whispers words
And sings like a bird
Happy in its nest.

Huangdi: "The principle of intercourse is not to ejaculate, or at least to save the semen, but what if one wishes to have children?"

Xuannü: "That depends on the age and state of health of the man concerned. But whatever his condition he must never force matters. A man of fifteen in good health can ejaculate several times a day, in average health once a day. A man of twenty in good health can ejaculate several times a day, in average health once a day. A man of thirty in good health can ejaculate once a day, in average health once every two days. A man of forty in good health may achieve ejaculation once every three days, in average health once every four days. A man of fifty in good health can ejaculate once every five days, in average health once every ten days. A man of sixty in good health may do so once every ten days, in average health, once every twenty days. A man of seventy in good health may do so every twenty days but if in only average health he should avoid ejaculation altogether. *Huangdi:* How much time should one allow to elapse between each act of love?

A man of twenty needs intercourse at least every four days, a man of thirty every eight days, a man of forty every sixteen days, a man of fifty every twenty-one days, a man of sixty may abstain, but if his health is good he can enjoy coitus once a month.

50

The battle of the sexes is like the art of war: before entering
the amorous lists the two opponents must be aware of their strengths
and weaknesses. On this depends the outcome of the battle.

Jou Pu Tuan

Cainü: "Tell me about intercourse with ghosts."

Pengzu: "Because of lack of intercourse or an excess of desire a man sometimes makes love to imaginary figures or ghosts. The pleasure derived from this kind of intercourse is much more intense than that from normal coitus. Such a man might well enjoy these experiences, conceal the matter from everybody else and take his secret with him to the grave. This disorder can be treated by unceasing intercourse night and day without ejaculation. Seven days later, at the most, the sufferer will be cured. If he is too weak for coitus, he must nevertheless achieve penetration, even if he cannot make any movements. If this disorder is not treated, the sufferer will die within a few years.

If the sceptic doubts the existence of this malady, let him go the mountains, the forest or the marshes in spring or fall and think of nothing else but intercourse. Three days later he will feel hot and cold by turns, experience anxiety and have visions (men see women, and women see men). The pleasure to be had from intercourse with such phantasms is more intense than that which comes from human love. This disorder is difficult to treat and arises from an attack of 'perverse energies' in the soul."

Little we mind the sinister flight of the crows!
Let us appreciate the benefits of reason:
So let us enjoy wine and pretty girls.

Kin P'ing Mei

Cainü: "What are the signs of weakness in a man?"

Pengzu: "When a man is in his prime, his Jade Stalk must be hot and his semen thick. If a man is weak, this is shown by five signs:

1. Energy deficiency: premature ejaculation.
2. Carnal deficiency: watery semen.
3. Sinew deficiency: semen with an offensive odor.
4. Osseous deficiency: spermatorrhea.
5. Physical deficiency: impotence.

These deficiencies are the result of brutal or abnormal intercourse. If they appear, have intercourse every day without ejaculation, and before a hundred days have passed, physical vigor will be increased a hundred times.

Sou Nu Fang

Huangdi questioned *Sunü* thus: "A man increases his energy through the way of Yin and Yang. But certain men who have practised it suffer from eye and ear disorders. Others who are harder hit feel physical weakness or impotence and can no longer follow the way of Yin and Yang. Tell me the cause of these problem."

Sunü replied as follows: "The problem raised by Your Imperial Majesty can happen to anyone. It can have various causes: intercourse with a woman advanced in years who is wearing her partner out; long abstinence from sex in the case of a man or mistaken techniques of intercourse, all these can cause *Qi Shang*. To enjoy long life one must not neglect these problems, but treat these disorders with medication the moment they appear.

Seven prohibitions should be observed, and if they are ignored the following pathological signs will appear:

1. Intercourse at the very beginning and very end of the moon, at full moon, during an eclipse of the sun or moon or during the five days of *Ding* will cause a weakening of the semen. The

Old, young, what does it matter so long as the Jade Stalk rises?

Gazing at the Hidden vessel results in desire as well as meditation.

man may also suffer from inpotence with a woman even when his Jade Stalk erects. His urine will be dark in color, he will suffer from spermatorrhea and he will die young.

2. A child conceived on a day of heavy rain or violent winds, storms or thunder, or when earth and the heavens tremble, will be mad, deaf-mute, feeble, forgetful or alternately timid and euphoric, depressed and disturbed.

3. Immediately after a meal the energy from the food consumed has not yet been distributed throughout the body and *Tai Cang* is still full. Hence the sexual act at this time risks harming the Six Bowels. The result will be dark or cloudy urine, blood in the urine, pains in the loins, contraction of the neck, oedema, feelings of distension in the epigastrum and loss of weight. The man will die before the age he could have reached if he had acted rightly.

4. Just after one has urinated, one's *Rong* energy (nutritive energy) and *Wei* (resistant energy) are not in their proper courses. Those who indulge in sexual intercourse at this time weaken their energies and will suffer from anorexia, feelings of distension in the abdomen, depression or anxiety, euphoria alternating with anger as seen in the insane and can suffer from painful periods.

5. Immediately after strenuous physical exertion or a long march the *Rong* energy (nutritive energy) is at a low level and the *Wei* energy (resistant energy) is not yet in its proper course. Coitus at this time harms the energies of the organs. Those affected suffer from intermittent choking sensations, dry lips, excessive sweating, indigestion, feelings of distension in the upper abdomen and weariness throughout the whole body.

6. Soon after a bath or considerable physical effort the body is wet with water or sweat. If the man catches a chill during intercourse, he will suffer from pains and contractions in the lumbar regions, shooting pains in the lower abdomen, tiredness of the limbs, reversal of the energy circulating to the organs, boils on the face or head.

7. If a man in the course of a conversation with a woman suddenly forces her to have sexual intercourse, the pilous system will expand, thus causing morbid energies to attack the organs. He will suffer from pains in the penis, seizure of the organs, deafness, cloudy vision, dyspnoea and seizure of the spleen. He can also become terror-stricken, forgetful or subject to fits of abstraction. This can also damage the health of women.

Sexual intercourse must be avoided at the times specified in the Seven Prohibitions. If this rule is broken, the person affected must apply a suitable remedy."

As the boat
Drifts with the stream
Springtime caresses
Are given and received.

Ju Fang Mi Ju

"Those who desire to increase their energy by the way of coitus must not have intercourse with only one girl. In fact it is preferable to make love to three, nine, eleven or even more, for the more partners there are the better will be the effect. Absorbing the woman's secretions strengthens the man's sperm. His skin and body become lighter, his sight becomes more acute, his strength and energy are so greatly increased that even an old man could recover the vigor he had at twenty. If the person concerned is young, his strength is multiplied by a hundred.

Change partners after every act, as this will prolong life. In fact if one always has intercourse with the same girl, her Yin diminishes and so, consequently, does the effect of coitus."

Quingniu Daoshi states: "The more one changes partners, the better the effect will be: ten girls in one night would be excellent. If one always makes love to the same girl, her secretions lose their strength, become incapable of benefiting the man and diminish."

Chonghezi says: "It is not only the Yang which can be nurtured, the Yin can be as well. For

In the Jade Pavillion
The banquet is over,
Intoxication leans its elbow on
Amorous desires.

Po Kin-Yi

66

example *Xiwangmu*, Empress of the West, followed the way of coitus. That is why, when she made love to a man, she destroyed him, while she herself bloomed and her countenance shone without recourse to *Zhifen*. She ate only milk products, played the five-stringed lute and enjoyed harmony of heart and body."

Xiwangmu had no consort, but she loved intercourse with young men. Of course she set a bad example to mankind, but she was not the only depraved woman in the world.

To desire good without evil, right without wrong, order without disorder shows that one does not understand the laws of the universe, for this is to long for heavens without an earth, a Yang without a Yin, a positive without a negative.

Tchouang Tseu

When a woman makes love with a man she must start by being completely calm and free from distractions. When desire comes, she must concentrate her mind and avoid sudden movement, in order to avoid using up her secretions. If that happened, the result would be ailments caused by cold and wind. If a woman who hears her partner making love to another woman becomes upset and jealous, her Yin energy becomes disturbed and can exhaust her secretions. Thus she risks growing old before her time and must therefore take great care.

*Though the nuns dare not
speak of it, at the bottom of
their hearts they are ready to yield.*

Ta Lo Fou

If a woman knows the way of fostering Yin, she harmonises the two energies. This harmony takes the form either of a child or of a quintessence which circulates through all the arteries of the body. Yang thus nourishes Yin and makes it possible to cure all disorders."

In the *Classic of the Immortal* it is written: "The method of *Huan Jing Bu Nao* (reversal of the sperm to invigorate the brain) must be practised at the moment when one feels the desire to ejaculate. For this purpose one uses two middle fingers of the left hand, pressing them between the scrotum and the anus while one exhales slowly and then brings one's teeth together twenty or thirty times without holding one's breath. The sperm cannot pass through the Jade Stalk and so returns to the brain." This method is the secret of the immortals and cannot be revealed to everyone.

If one wishes to be invigorated through sexual intercourse, one must lift up one's head, open one's eyes, look up, down and to left and right, tighten the stomach muscles, and hold one's breath at the moment of ejaculation. Thus the semen will be held back. If this method is followed, one can have sexual intercourse several times a day. If one ejaculates only twenty-four times a year one can live to be a hundred or two hundred and avoid all ailments and disorders."

What do girls dream of?

Dongxuanzi

"The heavens revolve to the left and the earth to the right. When spring and summer have passed, fall and winter follow on; the man sings and the woman accompanies him; those in authority take action, their subordinates obey—these are the fundamentals of existence.

If the man thrusts and the woman does not respond, or conversely if the woman makes her movements and the man does not respond, the effect is bad both for the man and the woman.

This sexual act is harmful because of the disharmony between Yin and Yang. In fact the principle of coitus is that when the man turns to the left, the woman turns to the right; when the man thrusts downwards, the woman pushes upwards. This is what is called celestial peace or terrestial joy.

One must pay careful attention to the difference between slight and deep penetration, speed or slowness of penetration and the east and west positions.

Slow movement must be like that of a carp playing with the fish-hook, whereas rapid movement must resemble a flock of birds battling against the storm-wind. Upward or downward, quick

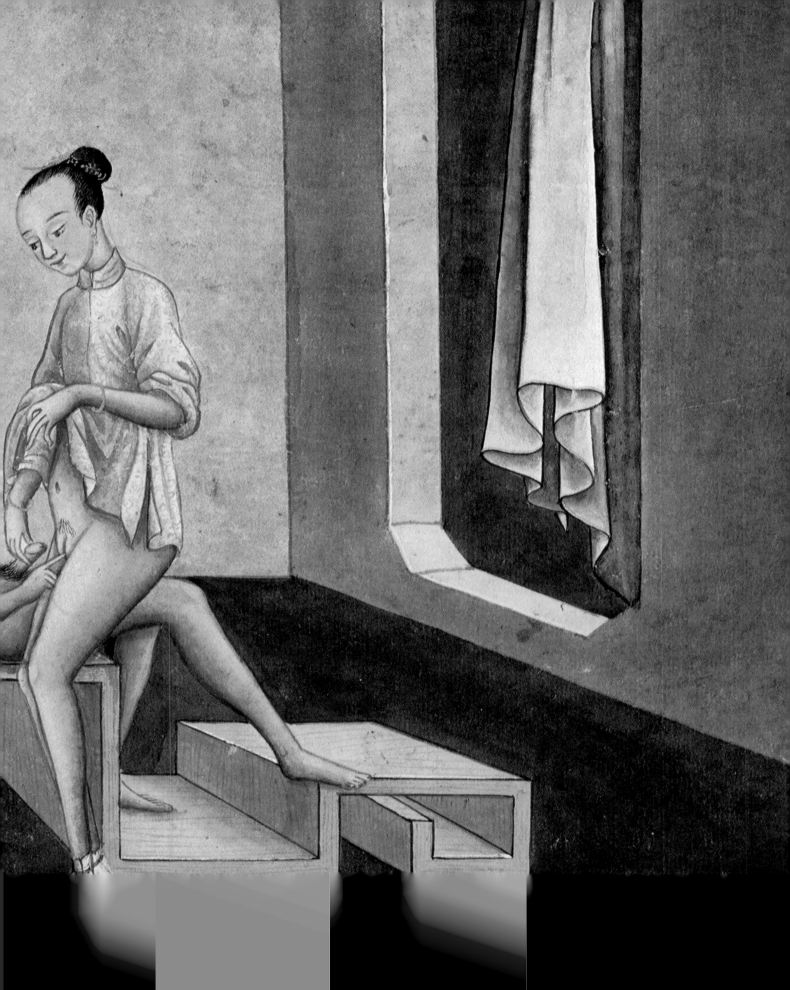

or slow penetration or withdrawal cannot be planned in advance, they must be decided on the spur of the moment.

Before beginning intercourse the man should sit on the left of the woman, so that she is on his right side. The man hugs the woman, holds her by the waist, caresses her body, speaks lovingly to her and holds her in an embrace which is sometimes tight and sometimes loose. With his mouth pressed against hers, the man sucks the woman's lower lip, whilst she sucks his upper lip. Saliva passes from one to the other whilst they gently nibble each other's tongue and lips, stroke each other's head and ears, then caress each other's upper body gently and lower body more passionately, and at this moment all troubles disappear.

Next the woman holds the man's Jade Stalk in her left hand, whilst he strokes her Jade Gate with his right hand. That is when the man feels Yin energy, his Jade Stalk rises like a mountain peak. The woman feels Yang energy and the secretions flow in her *Dan Xue* (Red Grotto, vagina) like a rushing stream in a deep valley. This phenomenon can only take place through the exchange of Yin and Yang energies, quite naturally and without outside intervention. This is the moment for intercourse. If the man does not feel this rising passion and the woman does not experience the release of her secretions, such exterior signs reveal an internal disorder."

Make love to more than one? Why hesitate
if harmony is thus created and pleasure shared?

Dongxuanzi: "When intercourse begins one should first sit, then recline, the man on the right and the woman on the left. A little while later the woman lies on her back, bends her legs and stretches out her arms. The man kneels between the woman's thighs and with his Jade Stalk touches her Jade Gate gently, like a firtree in front of the grotto. Then he sucks the woman's tongue and gazes first at her face and then at her *Jin Gou* (umbilicus). He caresses the skin between her breasts and her lower abdomen. At this stage he is excited and the woman entranced. Using his *Yang Feng* (penis) he moves upwards and downwards, positions himself more towards her umbilicus or towards the fold of her groin. When her secretions flow from her Red Grotto (vagina), *Yang Feng* penetrates *Zi Gong* (the Palace of the Child). The woman's lubrication rises to mosten *Shen Tian* (the Field of the Spirit) and flows down to nourish the lower depths. The woman is now utterly enraptured. Wiping the woman's pudenda with a piece of silk, again he introduces his Jade Stalk into the Red Grotto, penetrating nine times slightly and one deeply. Then he penetrates alternately quickly and slowly for the space of twenty-one breaths. When the woman's orgasm has begun, he thrusts and withdraws very quickly, and when she begins to move again he penetrates up to *Gu Shi*. The man turns to the right or to the left and when the woman's secretions flow again he must withdraw. He must not stay within, for that would be harmful to health: that must not be forgotten."

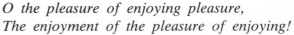

O the pleasure of enjoying pleasure,
The enjoyment of the pleasure of enjoying!

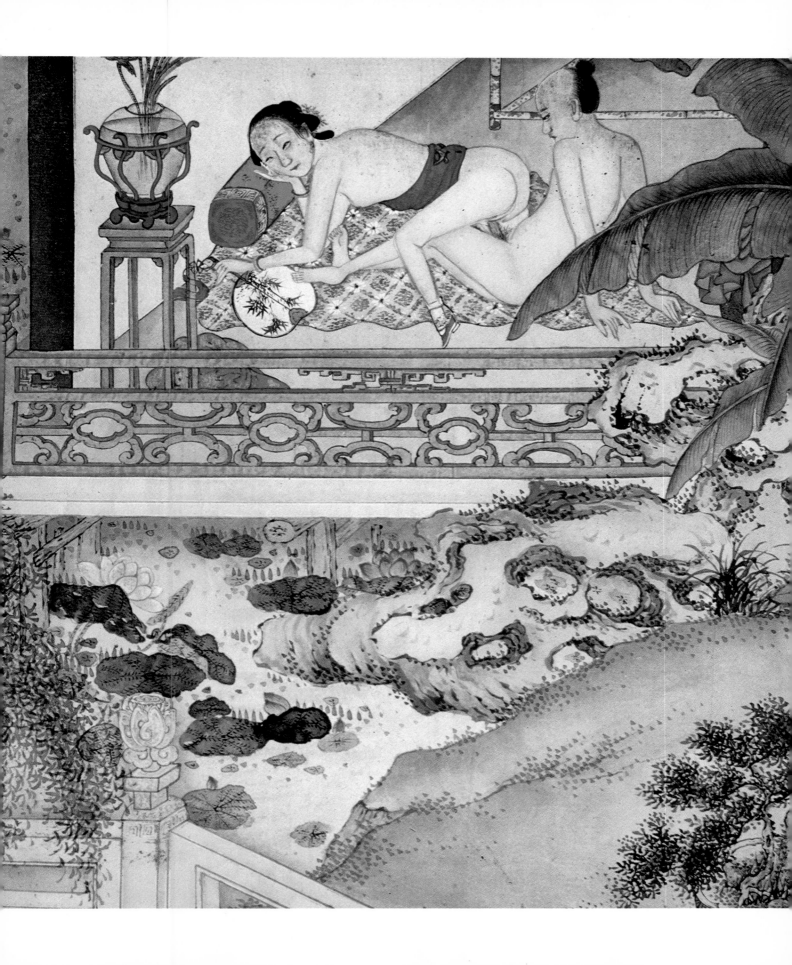

A mother is always split between her husband and her son:
what a lot of love she must pour out
for these insatiable beings!

Dongxuanzi: "According to the findings of research the number of positions for coitus does not exceed thirty. There are slight differences, but the basis is the same, whether for slight or deep penetration: reclining on the back or on the stomach. Here I suggest thirty positions for those who are learning the art of love:

1. *Xu Chou Mou:* (amorous conversation, a preparatory phase).
2. *Shen Qian Quan:* (avowal of love, a preparatory phase).
3. *Pu Sai Yu:* (the fish displays its gills to the sun).
4. *Qi Lin Tao:* (horn of *Qi Lin*).

These four phases consist of love-play without penetration.

5. *Can Chan Mian* (the intertwined silk worm): the woman lies on her back and puts her arms round the man's neck and with legs bent places her feet on his back. He kneels between her thighs, places his hands round her neck and then inserts his Jade Stalk.

6. *Long Wan Zhuan* (the nimble dragon twists and turns): the woman lies on her back with legs bent while the man kneels between her thighs. His left hand pushes the woman's legs up

80

towards her breasts, while with his right he guides his Jade Stalk into the Jade Gate.

7. *Yu Bi Mu* (fishes gazing at each other): both lovers lie on their sides, the woman places one leg on top of the man, who supports it and introduces his Jade Stalk.

8. *Yan Tong Xin* (the swallows are alike): the woman reclines on her back and stretches out her legs, the man lies on top of her and holds her round her neck while she grasps his waist and the Jade Stalk penetrates the Red Grotto.

9. *Fei Cui Jao* (the mating of the emerald): the woman lies on her back with legs bent. The man sits between her legs and encompasses her waist, then the Jade Stalk penetrates as far as *Qin Xuan*.

10. *Yuan Yan He* (the mating of the teal): the woman reclines on her side and bends her legs. The man lies behind her, places one leg over her lower thigh and then introduces his Jade Stalk.

11. *Kong Fan Die* (the butterfly turns a somersault in the air): the man reclines on his back and stretches out his legs. The woman sits as tride facing him supported on her hands and effects penetration herself.

Drinking the nectar of Yin
from the Jade Fountain by the light
of a flickering candle is pleasure shared.

One must wait
For the needle to thread itself.
Kin P'ing Mei

12. *Bei Fei Fu* (the wild duck flies away): The man lies on his back with legs extended. The woman faces his feet and lowers herself to bring about penetration.

13. *Yan Yi Song* (the reclining firtree): the woman lies with her legs in the air whilst the man encircles her waist and she his, so that the Jade Stalk enters the Jade Gate.

14. *Lin Tan Zhu* (the bamboo before the altar): both man and woman stand and kiss whilst the point of Yang penetrates the Red Grotto.

15. *Luan Shuan Wu* (the dance of the phoenix): one partner lies on top of the other. The partner underneath folds the legs over the one above, so that both Yins are opposite each other and each Jade can rub against the other.

16. *Feng Jiang Chu* (the phoenix protects its fledgling): a large, fat woman has intercourse with a little man.

17. *Hai Ou Xiang* (the flight of the gull): the man stands by the side of the bed, the woman raises her legs and the man inserts his Jade Stalk into her *Zi Gong* (Palace of the Child).

18. *Ye Ma Yue* (the leap of the wild horse): the woman reclines on her back, puts her feet on the man's right shoulder and then his Jade Stalk penetrates her Jade Gate.

84

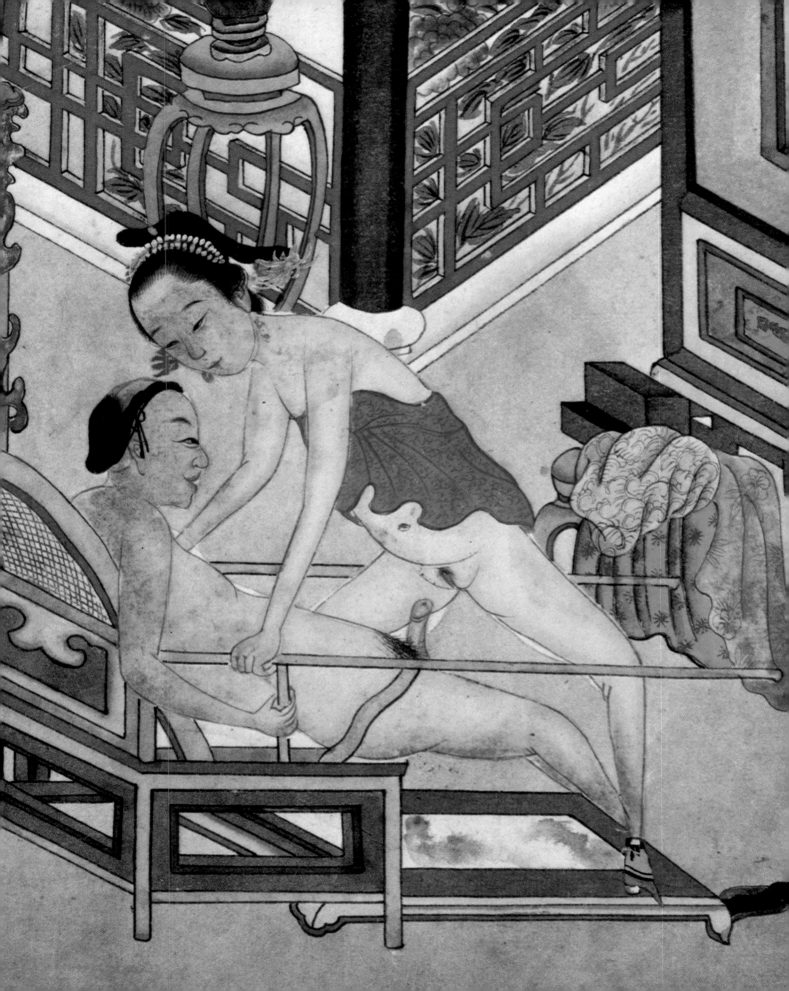

The Jade Stalk plunges passionately into the Red Grotto while delirious hands stroke the sweet places of scented bodies.

19. *Ji Cheng Zu* (the gallop of the thoroughbred horse): the woman lies on her back, the man squats and holds his partner's neck with his left hand her foot with his right hand. His Jade Stalk enters her *Zi Gong*.

20. *Ma Yao Ti* (the horse shakes his hoof): the woman reclines on her back, the man puts one of her feet on his shoulder whilst the other is bent, then his Jade Stalk is inserted into her *Zi Gong*.

21. *Bai Hu Teng* (the white tiger leaps): the woman kneels and lowers her head and torso. The man kneels behind her and penetrates *Zi Gong* with his Jade Stalk.

22. *Xuan Chan Fu* (the black cicada climbs up): the woman lies on her stomach with her legs spread. The man bends his legs, puts his hands around her neck and inserts his Jade Stalk from the rear.

23. *Shan Yang Dui Shu* (the goats climb the trees): the man is seated, the woman has her back to him and squats immediately above his Jade Stalk. The man takes her by the waist and quickly introduces his Jade Stalk.

24. *Kun Ji Lin Chuan* (the cicada heads for the field): the man is seated. One woman points the Jade Stalk towards her Jade Gate whilst another woman removes her skirt so that she can experience greater pleasure.

25. *Dan Xue Feng You* (the phoenix visits the red grotto): the woman lies on her back and uses her hands to hold her legs in the air. The man leans over the bed and inserts his Jade Stalk.

26. *Xuan Ming Peng Zhu* (the rock flies away over the black sea): the woman reclines on her back and places her feet on the man's shoulders. He holds her waist and introduces his Jade Stalk.

What wonderment, what heavenly pleasure is love's sweetness!

Mount the woman
Like a mare in rut.
Bestride the man
Like a galloping horse.

27. *Yin Yuan Bao Shu* (the monkey moans and clasps the tree): the man is seated, the woman sits on his thighs facing him and puts her arms around him. The man holds the base of the woman's spine with one hand and supports himself with the other.

28. *Mai Shu Tong Xue* (the cat and the mouse share the same hole): this position has two stages. In the first the man reclines on his back and stretches his legs out, whilst the woman lies on top facing him and inserts his Jade Stalk. In the second the woman lies on her stomach with the man on her back, so that his Jade Stalk finds her Jade Gate.

29. *San Chun Lu* (the donkey at the end of spring): the woman places her hands and feet on the bed. The man stands on the floor behind her, holds her by the waist and inserts his Jade Stalk in her Jade Gate.

30. *Qiu Gou* (the dog in the fall): the partners stand with their hands and feet touching the bed, each with the base of the spine touching that of the other. The man ducks down and thrusts his Jade Stalk into the woman's Jade Gate.

90

In love all is possible
If the partners are in harmony.

Dongxuanzi: "The Jade Stem can have nine modes. They are:
1. The Jade Stalk thrusts from left to right like a brave general.
2. It leaps up and comes down like a wild horse jumping over a chasm.
3. It moves in gentle, regular curves like seagulls following the waves.
4. It thrusts and withdraws like a crow pecking.
5. It penetrates deeply or skims over the surface like a stone thrown into water.
6. It penetrates gently and withdraws slowly like a snake returning to its nest.
7. It enters and then withdraws quickly like a scared mouse returning to its hole.
8. It surges upwards like an eagle which has just caught a hare.
9. It rises and falls like a junk struggling against a typhoon.

Two gates open up
To the desires
Of the lustful lord.

There are also six positions for intercourse:

1. Supporting the Jade Stalk to effect coitus: this is called "cutting the shell to take out the pearl".

2. The Jade Stalk moves down into *Yu Li* and moves up to *Jin Guo* (the umbilicus): "breaking the stone to find the jade".

3. The Jade Stalk thrusts down into *Xuan Tai* (the Jade Terrace): "ramming the iron rammer".

4. The Jade Stalk thrusts from left to right: "five hammers pounding the iron".

5. The Jade Stalk rubs against *Shen Tian* (Field of the Spirits): "the peasant plows his field".

6. *Xuan Pu* (Garden of Mystery) and *Tian Ting* (Celestial Court) rub against each other: "two shepherds come face to face".

Huangdi: « What are the *Wu Chang* (five virtues)? »

Sunü: « The calm stalk remains hidden »: its highest virtue is to give generously; the five virtues are: giving unstintingly, or *Ren* (benevolence); inner emptiness, *Yi* (equity); the knot at the end, *Li (etiquette);* when it wishes it rises, when it does not, it stops, this is *Xin* (faith); after the act it droops, this is *Zhi* (wisdom). One can discern a real man from the fact that he practises the *Wu Chang* (five virtues). If he gives in accordance with the virtue of *Ren* (benevolence), the quintessence will be wanting; the virtue of *Yi* (equity) requires that the jade stalk should be empty inside, whereas if it ejaculates the stalk will be full; the virtue of *Li* (etiquette) is a moderating influence, and the virtue of *Xin* (faith) is that of self-control. He who understands these five principles and practises them will know the path of intercourse and enjoy a long life. »

Tao has neither beginning nor end,
It exists of itself and by itself.
Before heaven and earth existed
It was through all eternity.

Tchouang Tseu